Written by

Peter Crawshaw

Consultant Dick Bloom

Illustrated by

Ann Savage

SILVER BURDETT PRESS
ENGLEWOOD CLIFFS, NEW JERSEY

Editors Steve Parker, Nigel Flynn, Sue Seddon
Editor, U.S. Edition Nancy Furstinger
Designers Bridget Morley, Patrick Nugent
Photo-researcher Hugh Olliff
Studio services Kenneth Ward

A TEMPLAR BOOK

Devised and produced by Templar Publishing Ltd
107 High Street, Dorking, Surrey RH4 1QA

Adapted and first published in the United States in 1988
by Silver Burdett Press, Englewood Cliffs, N.J.

Color separations by Positive Colour Ltd, Maldon, Essex
Printed by L.E.G.O., Vicenza, Italy

Library of Congress Cataloging-in-Publication Data

Crawshaw, Peter.
Australia.
(People & places)
"A Templar book" — Verso t.p.
Includes index.
Summary: Text and illustrations introduce "the land down under."
1. Australia — Juvenile literature. [1. Australia.] I. Savage, Ann, ill.
II. Title III. Series: People & places (Englewood Cliffs, N.J.)
DU96.C73 1988 919.4 88-18426
ISBN 0-382-09511-1

Contents

WHERE IN THE WORLD?

Australia is the sixth largest country in the world. It is both the biggest island and the smallest continent. It is situated in the Southern Hemisphere, which means its seasons are opposite to those of North America, Europe, and other parts of the Northern Hemisphere. For Australians, Christmas Day is in midsummer.

Australia's nearest neighbors are Papua New Guinea and Indonesia to the north, and New Zealand 1,250 miles to the southeast.

Australia is a country of great climatic and physical contrasts. The north is tropical because it is closer to the Equator than the south. It has a mostly warm and damp climate. Much of the south is temperate, with a Mediterranean-type climate. However, Australia is generally a dry land. It has more desert, in proportion to its area, than any other continent.

Despite its immense size, the population of Australia is only 16 million people. This is 234 million less than the population of the U.S., which is approximately equal in area to Australia.

KEY FACTS

- Australia's land area is 2,966,150 square miles. This is about four-fifths the area of the U.S.
- The country is divided into six self-governing states and two territories (see map opposite), one of which has now been given the status of self government. These are Queensland, South Australia, New South Wales, Victoria, Western Australia, Tasmania (an island), Northern Territory, and Australian Capital Territory (A.C.T.).
- The capital of Australia is Canberra in A.C.T., which has a population of nearly 300,000.
- The largest city is Sydney, with a population of nearly 3,500,000.
- The official religion of Australia is Christianity.
- Australia is known as "the land down under" because of its location.
- The currency is the Australian *dollar* ($). There are 100 *cents* (c) in one dollar.

Symbols of Australia

Australia's early links with the U.K. are shown in the national flag, which has the Union Flag in one corner. The Southern Cross stars and the southern Pole Star also are shown as both can only be seen in the skies of the Southern Hemisphere.

This coat of arms is used by the Government of Australia. The shield in the center contains six badges, each representing one of the six states. The shield is supported by a kangaroo and emu, well-known Australian animals.

Hot and hostile land

Much of the Gibson Desert is covered by small, flat, red stones called "gibbers". Because of this it is sometimes called the "Gibber Desert". The rocks are rusty-red because they contain iron. In this hostile region, where few people live, summer temperatures regularly soar to 105°F.

Guide to states and territories

1 Western Australia
2 Northern Territory
3 South Australia
4 Queensland
5 New South Wales
6 Victoria
7 Australian Capital Territory
8 Tasmania

The first Australians

The Aboriginal people came to Australia at least 40,000 years ago, from Southeast Asia. When the first Europeans arrived, 200 years ago, the Aboriginals' way of life changed drastically (see page 28).

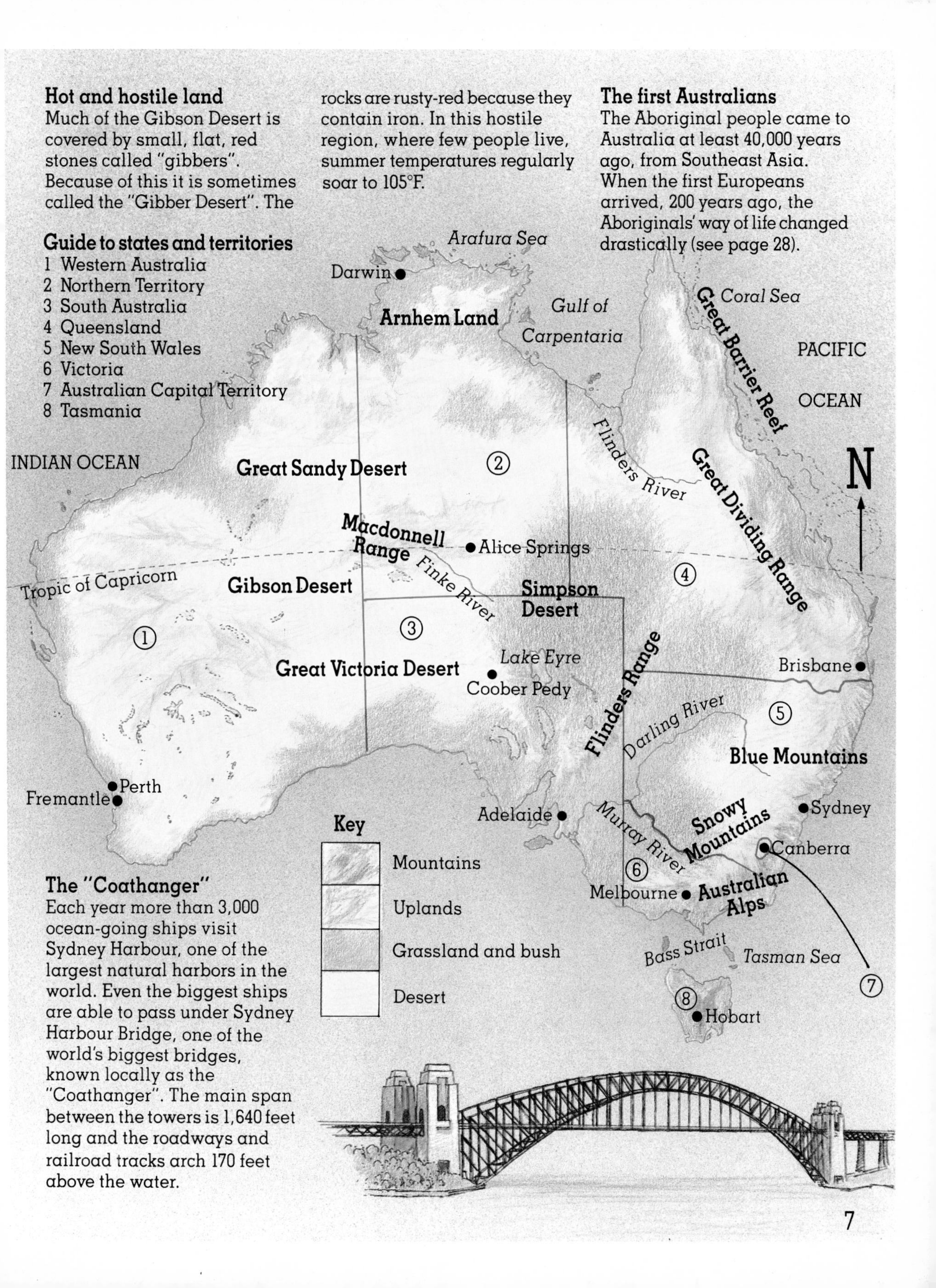

The "Coathanger"

Each year more than 3,000 ocean-going ships visit Sydney Harbour, one of the largest natural harbors in the world. Even the biggest ships are able to pass under Sydney Harbour Bridge, one of the world's biggest bridges, known locally as the "Coathanger". The main span between the towers is 1,640 feet long and the roadways and railroad tracks arch 170 feet above the water.

THE DRIEST CONTINENT

Australia is the world's driest continent. More than two-thirds of the country, mostly in the center and west, is desert or dry, scrubby bush land (wilderness). In some places it does not rain for years. The climate is intensely hot and the thin, dusty soil is unsuitable for growing crops. In the summer months of December to March, the temperature at Alice Springs, in central Australia, often exceeds 100°F for days on end.

However, Australia is so large that there are many different types of climate and vegetation. In the tropical region, along the northern coast, the summers are hot and wet. Darwin has an average rainfall approaching 40 inches a year (New York City's average is 41 inches). Most rain falls in the summer months, and the average January temperature is 82°F.

South Australia has mild, wet winters. In the southwest the summers are hot and dry – Perth's average January temperature its 73°F and its average yearly rainfall is 17 inches. Southeastern Australia has a temperate climate. The average summer temperature in Sydney is 72°F, and 55°F in winter.

KEY FACTS

- ▶ One-third of Australia has less than 10 inches of rain each year.
- ▶ The hottest place in Australia is Marble Bar, in the west, which has recorded temperatures over 100°F for more than five months during the summer of 1923-24.
- ▶ Australia is a relatively flat country with mountains only in the eastern regions. Mount Kosciusko, Australia's tallest mountain, between Sydney and Melbourne, is 7,308 feet high.
- ▶ Native Australian trees, such as the eucalyptus, do not change color during the year. They are evergreens and do not shed their leaves in winter.

Coping with the heat
In the hot climate of north Australia, most houses are built with verandas (roofed porches) which provide shade. In houses where there is no air-conditioning, people sleep outside on the veranda in summer, where it is often cooler.

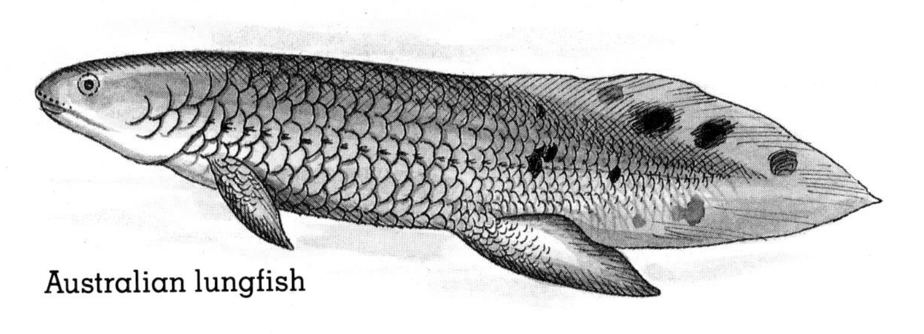

Australian lungfish

Billabong creatures

The Aboriginal word *billabong* means "dead river". It is usually used to describe a river or water hole that contains water for only part of the year. A rainstorm may bring a flood, filling the billabongs, but in the intense heat the water soon dries up. In the Burnett and Mary Rivers, in northern Queensland, live Australian lungfish. These creatures have developed both gills and lungs so that they can survive buried in the mud when the rivers partially dry up and become slow-flowing in the summer.

Hidden water source

Deep beneath the deserts of central and western Australia lie hidden reserves of water. To tap this, water pumps have been sunk. Wind sails (windmills) on top of towers provide power to pump up the water. Unfortunately, much of this water is too impure for people to drink, although it can be used by animals.

Flooded desert

Although parts of Australia have severe droughts, other areas suffer from floods. In 1974 the Brisbane area of Queensland had huge floods, as shown here. In 1806 the level of the Hawkesbury River at Richmond, 31 miles northwest of Sydney, rose by a phenomenal 92 feet!

THE TEMPERATE SOUTH

Most Australians live in the temperate southern part of the country, especially near the southeast coast, where winters are mild and the summers are sunny and warm. The first Europeans who came to Australia, in 1788, settled in the southeast where the climate was similar to the one they had left behind. Within 100 years, much of the land was cleared for sheep and wheat farming. Today wool, lamb, and wheat are among Australia's main exports.

Not all of the original vegetation has been cleared. National Parks have been established in New South Wales, Victoria, and the island state of Tasmania (150 miles south of Melbourne). Here, wildlife is protected and people from the cities can enjoy camping vacations and nature walks.

The island of Tasmania is slightly larger than West Virginia. It has rugged mountains, rolling land, deserted beaches, and impenetrable forests. It was once the home of the thylacine, or Tasmanian tiger.

Harnessing the snow
About 60 miles south of the capital city, Canberra, are the Snowy Mountains. In winter, more snow falls there than falls over the whole of Switzerland. In the mountains, several dams have been built as part of a hydroelectric plan which harnesses the melted snow and heavy rain from the mountains, to provide power and to regulate the water for irrigation.

The oldest trees

Huon pines are some of the longest-living trees in the world. A few are believed to be 2,000 years old. They grow in the rain forests of the Huon Valley in southern Tasmania. Much of the forest has been cleared to make room for fruit plantations. Two-thirds of Tasmania's fruit is grown here, and vast quantities of apples are exported each year, principally to the United Kingdom.

Extinct "tiger"?

The thylacine (Tasmanian tiger) is a rare marsupial (see page 14) that is now thought to be extinct. More like a wolf, it is 3 feet long, with a striped coat and long tail. Despite rumors, no thylacines have been seen alive since 1933. These animals were hunted, since they attacked sheep and chickens. However, it is possible that a few still survive in Tasmania's dense forests.

THE TROPICAL NORTH

The tropical lands of northern Australia do not have four seasons, like the south. They have only two seasons – "wet" and "dry". The wet season, November to April, is hot and humid. Heavy monsoon rain turns large areas of the Northern Territory and Queensland into vast temporary lakes, which attract thousands of birds in seach of food and nesting grounds.

In the dry season, May to October, the temperature on the Queensland coast averages 70°F. With long spells of dry, sunny weather this region, particularly the Great Barrier Reef, has become popular with Australians from the south, who are in search of a "winter" vacation.

The Great Barrier Reef is a chain of 500 islands and coral reefs, 1,250 miles long, off the coast of northeast Queensland. It is one of the natural wonders of the world. The Reef is home to some 400 kinds of coral and 1,500 types of fish. Turtles, stingrays, and sea anemones abound in its beautifully clear, warm waters. Snorkling is popular with tourists, although with sharks and poisonous coneshells, lionfish, and jellyfish, danger lurks just below the surface.

Catastrophic cyclones
One of the hazards of living on the coast of northern Australia is the storms and winds of the cyclone. A cyclone is an area of very low air pressure with very strong winds revolving around it, which can cause great damage. On Christmas Day 1974 a cyclone with winds of 135 miles an hour damaged or destroyed nearly all Darwin's buildings, as shown above, causing mass evacuation.

Kakadu National Park
Kakadu is one of the five parts of Australia included in the World Heritage List for areas of outstanding natural beauty. Its area is 4,800 square miles, which is about the size of Connecticut, and is situated near Darwin. It preserves all the natural features of the tropical north – grasslands, river gorges, swamps, steep-cliffed valleys, and abundant wildlife. It is also home to large crocodiles, as shown here.

Newcastle Bay

Cape York Peninsula

THE GREAT BARRIER REEF

Princess Charlotte Bay

Lizard Island

Cooktown

Trinity Bay

Cairns

Dunk Island

Flinders Passage

Halifax Bay

Townsville

Whitsunday Island

Repulse Bay

Brampton Island

Broad Sound

Great Keppel Island

Keppel Bay

- Parts of the Great Barrier Reef are 10,000 years old.
- The reef is 1,250 miles long, making it the largest coral reef in the world.
- There are really two reefs: an outer reef, which is still growing, and an inner reef on which many islands and coral islands are situated.
- In the 1960s and '70s, large parts of the reef were eaten away by the crown-of-thorns starfish, which increased in numbers.
- The number of starfish has fallen in recent years and the reef is no longer under threat.
- The starfish may be a natural hazard, or its numbers may be affected by even slight changes in the level of pollution. Researchers are working to find the reason.

What is coral?

The shining red, yellow, blue, pink, and brown colors that make up the Great Barrier Reef come from tiny creatures called coral polyps. Each polyp is a tiny anemone-like animal that builds a crusty limestone cup, attached to other polyps, as a protective shield. When the animal dies, the cup is left. Millions of cups slowly build up into the rocks that make the reef. The polyps feed at night, wafting their stinging tentacles in the water to capture their prey.

Stagshorn coral

Fern coral

Brain coral

ANIMALS IN DANGER

The continent of Australia has been cut off from other land masses for 50 million years. During this time, its wildlife has evolved in a unique way. In no other continent are there so many kinds of marsupials – mammals that carry their young in a pouch on their abdomens until they can fend for themselves. Some, like the kangaroo and wallaby, have pouches that open at the top. Others, such as the koala and wombat, have pouches that open at the bottom.

When the early European settlers arrived in the late 18th century they brought with them cattle, sheep, rabbits, foxes, dogs, rats, and cats. These animals upset the existing ecological balance. Before numbers were reduced by the disease myxomatosis in the 1950s, rabbits numbered hundreds of millions in Australia. In about 1952 it was estimated that they were consuming vast areas of pasture – grazing land that could have sustained 25 million sheep.

As the land was cleared for farming, many native animals were killed. Kangaroos were hunted and millions were shot for leather and pet food, although the export of kangaroo meat was banned in 1973. Even so, kangaroos survive in their millions, mainly in northern and central Australia.

Small and cuddly
Before the hunting of koalas was banned in 1930, millions of these inoffensive creatures were slaughtered for their fur. Today they are protected and their numbers are increasing. Koala "bears" are not true bears, they are marsupials. In the wild they live for up to 20 years. They feed on the leaves of only a few varieties of the eucalyptus tree, from which they also get most of the water they need. Baby koalas spend the first six months of life in their mother's pouch, then cling to her back for several months.

Sand goannas
The sand goanna can grow up to 7 feet long. It lives in desert regions and eats rabbits, other lizards, eggs, and insects. Unusual for a lizard, it has a neck which enables it to turn its head and look in any direction. There are 300 different kinds of lizard in Australia.

The "Roos"

The kangaroo is unique to Australia. There are, in fact, some 90 kinds of kangaroos and wallabies (the name for some small species of brightly colored kangaroo). The smallest is the rat kangaroo, which stands only 6 inches high. The biggest is the red kangaroo (shown here), a threatened species which can grow taller than a person and weigh 200 pounds. When chased, the red kangaroo can bound along at a speed of 40 miles per hour. At birth a young kangaroo, or "joey", measures a mere half an inch.

FLOWERS, TREES, AND BIRDS

Many visitors to Australia are surprised by the spectacular colors of the country's wild flowers. Perhaps the brightest hued species are the crimson waratah (the floral emblem of New South Wales), the kangaroo paw (native to Western Australia), the Sydney flannel flower, the orange grevillea, and the blue cleocarpusm, found in the tropical forests of the north. But not all the country's many thousands of wild flowers have yet been studied. In Western Australia alone (the "wild flower" state) there are 6,000 varieties of wild flowers, some of which grow only in this region.

Australia's forests are limited to coastal areas where the rainfall is heaviest. In the north there are dense rain forests with trees like the kauri pine, which grow more than 165 feet tall. In the subtropical and temperate forests farther south, the giant mountain ash (eucalyptus), one of the world's tallest trees, reaches heights of 400 feet.

The two most common Australian trees are the wattle (acacia), whose yellow flowers feature on the country's coat of arms, and the eucalyptus, or "gum" tree. There are more than 500 different kinds of gums found all over the continent.

The "laughing jackass"
One of Australia's best-known birds is the kookaburra. Its call is very like a particularly loud laugh, earning it the nickname "laughing jackass". Kookaburras are members of the kingfisher group of birds, and live mainly in forests. The kookaburra is, however, often seen in towns, scavenging for slugs and snails.

Kangaroo paw

Crimson waratah

Sydney flannel flower

"Gum" trees

Wherever you travel in Australia you see eucalyptus or "gum" trees, named because of the sticky substance that oozes from the bark. Different types of eucalyptus are often classified by their bark. Ironbark has a dark, deeply furrowed, and very tough bark; stringybark is brown, loose, and fibrous. Gum trees are very resilient, able to survive the forest fires which are an ever-present danger. By clearing the ground of undergrowth and other trees, the fire destroys other competitors for water and light. The photograph above shows snow gums, named after their white trunks.

The bird that cannot fly

Australia has more than 800 species of birds, including the emu, paradise parakeet, and budgerigar. The emu, found on open grassland all over Australia, is the world's second-largest bird after the ostrich. A fully-grown emu can weigh 110 pounds and stand taller than a person. It has an ungainly walk, but it can run at a speed of 30 miles an hour.

GOING "OUTBACK"

The center of Australia is formed from very old rocks and is one of the most ancient landscapes on Earth. It is called the "outback" or the "red center". The name "outback" originated when people living on the coast set off to travel into the vast interior, saying "I'm going out back". Red is the main color because the soil contains iron oxide which is rusty in color.

The deserts and scrub land of the outback are vast, covering more than two-thirds of Australia. The land is mostly flat and isolated – fewer than 100,000 people live there. The railroad from Sydney to Perth (about 2,200 miles) has a stretch of almost 310 miles without a single bend – the longest piece of straight railroad track in the world.

In the heart of the interior is Alice Springs. It is the largest settlement in the outback, but even so has only 25,000 residents. Air travel, radio, telephone, television, and tourism have helped to make the people of the outback feel less isolated. But it is still a hostile land. Each year, a few ill-prepared city dwellers drive into the interior and die because of lack of water.

The "Rock"

The sandstone of Uluru rears out of the desert near Alice Springs, like a prehistoric monster. Known until 1985 as Ayers Rock, Uluru is 1,140 feet high and more than 5 miles round at the base. It is a place of mystery and great beauty, particularly at sunset when it changes color from yellow to gold, red, and finally purple. Around the base of the rock there are many caves decorated with Aboriginal paintings. To the Pitjantjatjara people, who have been acknowledged as owning Uluru, it is a sacred place.

A town called Alice

Alice Springs is almost in the very center of Australia. Founded in about 1870, it was for many years a small settlement of miners, traders, and visiting Aboriginals from the surrounding deserts. Then, it was just a handful of shacks but in the past 20 years, it has become a center for tourism with new hotels and shops. Sightseers fly into its airport and go on bushwalks and visits to Uluru rock, 275 miles to the southwest.

Baob tree, a familiar sight in the outback, whose wide trunk stores water for many years

Katherine Gorge

About 995 miles north of Alice Springs lies Katherine Gorge, near the town of Katherine. It is one of Australia's most popular scenic spots. Boats filled with tourists journey down the Katherine River between 200-foot high canyon walls. The gorge is rich in wildlife. Fig trees, wild flowers, and ferns grow out of the rock face. There are flying foxes, many exotic birds, and crocodiles on the banks of the deep, cool river.

SHEEP TO THE HORIZON

It once was said that Australia "rode on the sheep's back". This was true in a sense, because sheep farming brought great wealth to Australia, and today sheep wool and meat remain two of the main exports. New South Wales and Victoria are the major sheep-farming states, and contain more than half the country's sheep.

Sheep farms, or "stations" as they are called, are huge. Some are 600 square miles in area (twice the size of Kansas City), with as many as 30,000 sheep. Sheep dogs, bred from English and Scottish breeds, can do the work of three people in rounding up the large flocks of sheep, for shearing or taking to market.

In the drier areas of northern and central Australia there are even larger beef cattle ranches, or "runs". A few of these are each as large as the whole of England. "Blue-heeler" Australian cattle dogs are used to round up the cattle, although on some of the stations (ranches) helicopters are now used. Large trucks pulling several trailers, called "land trains", take the cattle many hundreds of miles to sale yards or slaughterhouses. Australian beef is exported all over the world.

KEY FACTS

- There are some 150 million sheep in Australia. This is one-fifth of the total number of sheep in the world.
- Australian sheep produce 800,000 tons of fleece each year, about one-quarter of total world wool production.
- One-quarter of Australia is occupied by several thousand cattle runs or stations, each averaging 120 square miles.
- Drought can drastically reduce the cattle population. A long drought during the 1970s reduced the number of cattle from 32 million in 1971 to 26 million in 1981.

Cattle "land train" on the highway

Australia's "cowboys"

Rounding up cattle on some large runs is still done by farmhands on horseback, called "drovers". Drovers can be away from home for weeks on end while rounding up cattle on a big ranch. At night they sleep in out-stations, or huts. Branding cattle with their owner's mark is an important part of the work on stations that are too big to be fenced. Newborn calves must be found so that they too can be stamped with the station's branding mark.

The shearing shed

Every sheep station has a shearing shed where the wool can be shorn from many sheep at the same time. A shearing team arrives at a station and may stay for several weeks, depending on the number of sheep to be shorn. The best shearer in the team is called a "ringer". The fleece is shorn in one piece using electric shears. It is graded according to quality, put into a large sack, and sent to the wool market to be sold.

Tough and durable

The Spanish merino, first introduced in 1797, is the main breed of sheep in Australia, accounting for three-quarters of the livestock. The merino is suited to a warm, dry climate. It is docile and hardy, able to withstand very dry conditions, and produces good quality wool.

INDUSTRY – EXPORTS AND IMPORTS

Australia is one of the world's leading industrialized nations. Its manufacturing industry developed after 1945 and now employs about one-quarter of the country's working people. As in other industrial countries, service industries also have grown to become the largest employer. Two-thirds of the working population of Australia have jobs in offices, stores, banks, schools, universities, and government departments. Fewer than one in 10 works in agriculture.

Food processing is the biggest manufacturing industry, in terms of both value and employment. This is followed by machinery, cars, aircraft, and shipbuilding. In the past 10 years the production of steel, aluminum, refined copper, lead, zinc, and tin has expanded rapidly and now accounts for one-quarter of all Australia's exports.

The most industrialized states are New South Wales and Victoria; the least industrialized are Western Australia and the Northern Territory. Before World War II, the United Kingdom was Australia's main trading partner, but in recent years trade has increased with Japan and the United States. These countries have invested heavily in Australian industry and are now its main trading partners. They are followed by New Zealand, West Germany, Singapore, and the Soviet Union.

Steel-making plant
Newcastle is built on a former mangrove swamp at the head of the Hunter River in New South Wales. It is one of the biggest metal-manufacturing plants in the Southern Hemisphere. Coal from the Hunter Valley is used to produce steel from iron ore mined at Iron Knob, in South Australia, and Yampi Sound in Western Australia.

Australia's first mass-produced car, the 1948 Holden

Industry threatened by competition
Manufacturing industries, such as car factories and steel mills, became increasingly important to Australia's economy after World War II. But the country has been faced with increasing competition from Southeast Asian countries since the 1970s, particularly in the clothing industry. Australia has imposed taxes on imported goods in order to make them more expensive and so protect its own industries.

Giant storage shed for wheat, New South Wales

A great granary

Australia is the third largest wheat-exporting nation in the world, after the U.S.A. and Canada. New South Wales and Western Australia are the main wheat-growing areas and together produce 18 million tons of wheat each year. More than half is exported, mainly to the U.S.A., Japan, and China.

Main wheat-growing areas

Perth

Sydney

Wine from the vine

In recent years, Australia has developed its grape-growing industry and has built up a reputation for producing good-quality wines. The climate of the southeast, with its very warm summers, is ideal for grape vines. This vineyard is in the Hunter Valley, near the coalmining area mentioned above left.

MINING, METALS, AND MINERALS

The outback is not just cattle-grazing country and vast empty space. Much of Australia's exporting wealth comes from the mining areas of the Northern Territory, Western Australia, and New South Wales. Deep under the red earth lie huge deposits of iron ore, bauxite (used to make aluminum), coal, silver, lead, zinc, copper, gold, crude oil, diamonds, and opals!

Weipa, in Queensland, has the largest reserves of bauxite in the world. And in the Pilbara region of Western Australia, huge open-cast mines produce iron ore, mainly for use in the U.S.A. and Japan.

But perhaps the most extraordinary mining town is Coober Pedy, 600 miles northwest of Adelaide, South Australia. It is the center of possibly the world's largest opal field. Its Aboriginal name means "man who lives in a hole". Today most of the town's population live in houses dug out of the hillside, to escape the intense heat. In Coober Pedy it can be 120°F for days on end.

Not everyone, however, is happy with the discovery of rich minerals in the outback. Many people fear that the building of mines and new mining towns will mean the destruction of a wild and beautiful land.

Mining "down under"
There are two types of mining in Australia: "open-cut" or open-cast, and shaft mining. This iron ore mine at Iron Monarch in the Middleback Ranges, South Australia, is an open-cut mine. This means that the iron ore is extracted from massive trenches dug into the ground. Although it is the most economic way of mining iron ore, it has resulted in a deeply-scarred landscape. Trucks follow the zigzag road down to the bottom where they collect the ore.

What are opals?
Almost all the world's opals are found in Australia. Millions of years old, opals are gemstones made of silica. They are valued for their colorful appearance, which is produced when they reflect light at different angles (as shown above). The photograph on the left shows the inside of an underground home in Coober Pedy, in the heart of the opal mining region.

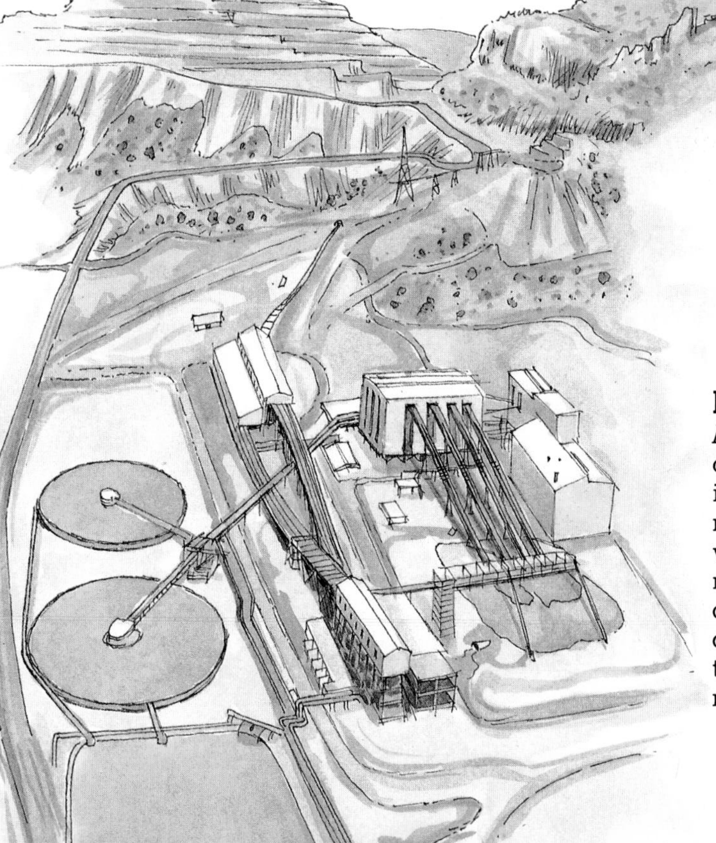

Diamonds are forever

At Argyle, 1,370 miles northeast of Perth in Western Australia, is one of the largest and most modern diamond mines in the world. Opened in 1985, the mine cost $430 million to develop and is designed to be able to extract three million tons of diamond-containing rocks each year.

ACROSS A VAST LAND

The vast size of Australia, and the dry, inhospitable interior, made traveling across the continent very difficult in the past. Today, several long-distance roads and railroads cross the outback. People who wish to "see Australia" may spend days driving from Sydney to Perth, a distance of about 2,200 miles, or from Melbourne to Darwin, which is about 1,900 miles. For hundreds of miles the roads have no service stations or settlements, so motorists must be well prepared.

Air travel has become very important in recent years, and has helped the country to "shrink" in size. A flight from Perth to Sydney takes four to five hours. Alice Springs, in the center of the interior, can be reached in three to four hours from any major city.

Small airplanes have become vital for outback life. They carry supplies and passengers between airstrips in towns and on sheep stations and cattle ranches. In remote homesteads the weekly flight, carrying mail, groceries, magazines and books, spare parts for machinery, and other goods, is eagerly awaited by the whole family.

Cars crowded together
Much of Australia is uninhabited. Yet in densely populated areas near the coast, people and cars are crowded together and there are traffic jams just like in any big city. Australians own some eight million cars, and there are more than half a million trucks. Drivers sometimes say that they are all right here, in Sydney's rush-hour traffic!

Camels in the outback?
During the last century, hundreds of camels were taken to Australia. They were well suited to carrying goods and people through the hot, harsh lands of the interior, and they were used by miners and explorers such as Burke and Wills (page 33). When trains and cars became more common some camels were set free. They survived and bred in the desert regions, and now they roam wild. Today, camels are reared also on farms and tamed to act as pack animals on sightseeing treks through the outback. Each year people in Alice Springs organize a "Camel Cup" race meeting – although the atmosphere is one of fun rather than serious competition!

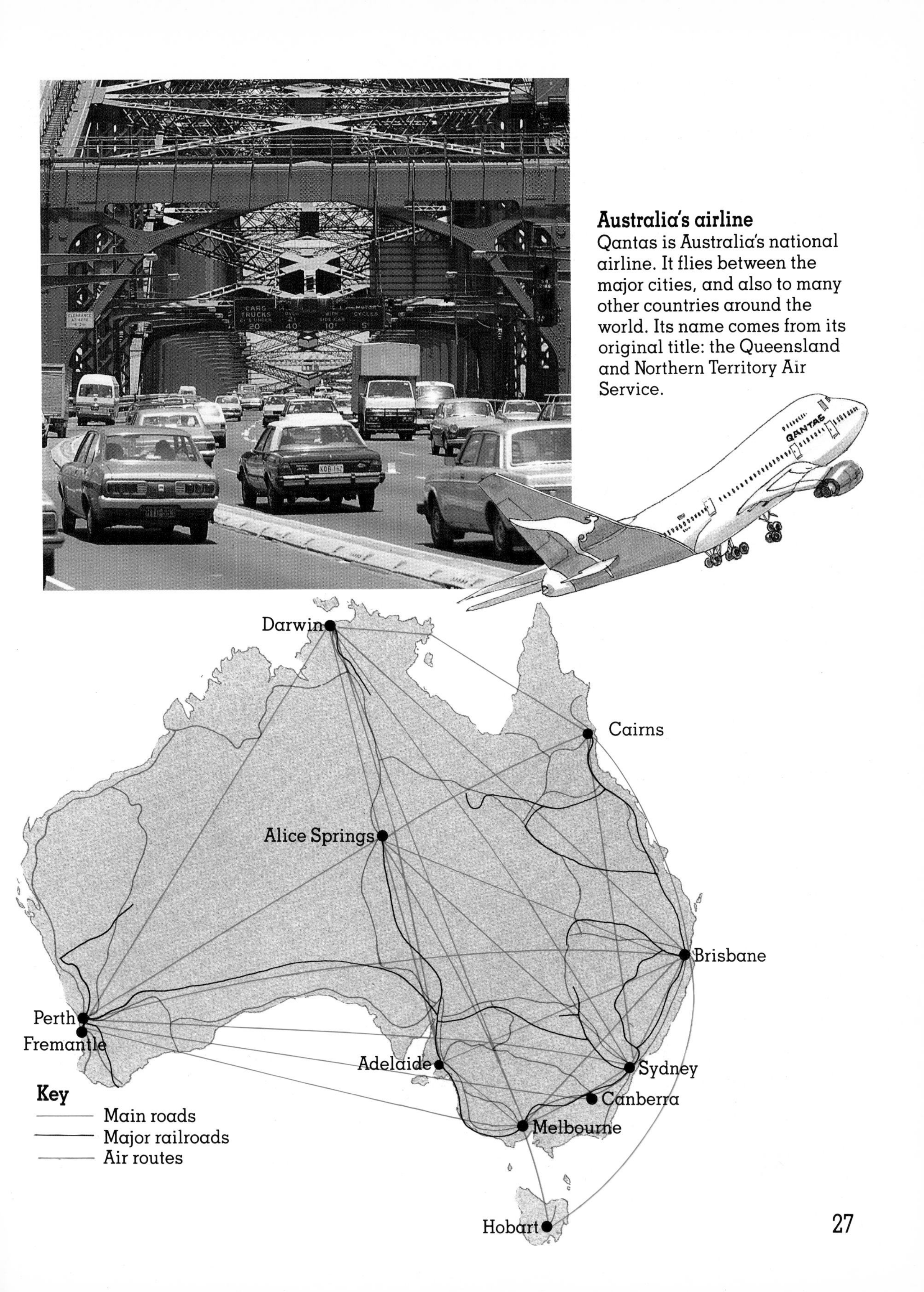

Australia's airline

Qantas is Australia's national airline. It flies between the major cities, and also to many other countries around the world. Its name comes from its original title: the Queensland and Northern Territory Air Service.

THE FIRST AUSTRALIANS

When the first European settlers arrived in Australia in 1788, the country was inhabited by some 300,000 people called Aboriginals. Their ancestors had come, 40,000 years or more ago, across a land bridge from Southeast Asia. Continents continually move, and as Australia slowly separated from Southeast Asia between 8,000 and 6,000 years ago the land bridge was covered by the sea, turning Australia into an island continent.

The Aboriginals lived a mostly peaceful, nomadic life, moving from one area to another when food became scarce. They gathered fruit, nuts, grubs and termites to eat, and hunted kangaroos and emus with stone-tipped or bone-tipped spears. They adapted to the harsh land without changing it too much.

With the coming of the European settlers, the way of life of the Aboriginals changed dramatically. Many were driven from their lands. Thousands died from European diseases against which they had no natural resistance. Their numbers dwindled. In Tasmania, none of the Aboriginals survived. Aboriginal land rights have become an important issue only in recent years, and their way of life has now begun to be respected.

"Dreamtime"
Many Aboriginal groups have deeply-felt beliefs, and central to their way of life is the concept of "the Time of Dreaming" or "Dreamtime". This is the time of the creation, when the land, sea, sky and all creatures were made. Many of these beliefs were recorded in rock paintings and carvings, as shown above. They also have been passed on from generation to generation by storytelling and through song and dance.

Australia's wild dogs
Dingoes are wild dogs of the outback, believed to have been brought to Australia by the Aboriginals thousands of years ago. They are expert hunters, eating almost anything they can catch – rabbits, sheep, cattle, snakes, even kangaroos. Although generally shy of humans, some dingoes are trained as hunting dogs by Aboriginals.

A corroboree

Corroborees are Aboriginal dances. The dancers wear special clothes and makeup. They are accompanied by drums and other percussion instruments, and by didgeridoos, drone-pipes made from long hollow bamboo stems that are extremely difficult to play. Corroborees form an important part of Aboriginal life. They are sometimes performed to persuade the spirits of their ancestors to bring rain, or to ensure successful hunting. Other corroborees are held to mark the time when boys reach manhood, to mourn a death or to celebrate love.

Woomera

Aboriginal hunting

Boomerangs are of two kinds, returning and non-returning. Contrary to popular belief, the non-returning boomerang is used for hunting. The crescent-shaped one that returns to the thrower is really a toy, used for amusement. The woomera is a spear-thrower, used as an extension of the thrower's arm. It has a hooked end into which the spear fits. An expert using a woomera can hurl a spear 100 feet with great accuracy. The nulla-nulla is a heavy wooden club, sometimes beautifully decorated by using a hot stone to burn in a pattern.

Ways of throwing a returning boomerang

CONVICTS AND SETTLERS

Long before the Europeans reached Australia, seafaring traders from Southeast Asia visited the country. Chinese maps 2,500 years old show parts of northern Australia. In 1642, Abel Tasman, a Dutchman, landed on present day Tasmania. The English naval captain James Cook landed on the east coast of Australia in 1770 and claimed the region for Britain's King George III.

For a century, England had sent convicts (convicted criminals) to its colonies, such as America. However, with American independence in 1783, Australia became the new "dumping ground" for the convicts and their families. The first European settlers in Australia included about 1,000 convicts who arrived in Australia in January 1788.

Between 1788 and 1860, when the practice was stopped, 160,000 convicts were sent to Australia. Life there was hard and conditions were harsh. But from the 1820s the outback began to be cleared by freed convicts, ex-prison guards, and newly arrived settlers. Sheep and wheat farms were established and the settlers were ready to explore the vast interior.

On the Rocks
The convict barracks in the historic Rocks area in Sydney recently have been restored and have become a tourist attraction. They were built in 1819, and 600 convicts slept there each night, after breaking stones and building roads during the day.

67,980 male convicts and 12,460 female convicts sent to New South Wales between 1787 and 1840

54,640 male convicts and 12,500 female convicts sent to Tasmania between 1803 and 1853

9,688 male convicts sent to Western Australia between 1850 and 1866

Transported for life
The men and women on the convict ships had been sentenced to "transportation for life", and they knew they would never see Britain again. Few were hardened criminals – most were guilty of crimes such as stealing, receiving stolen goods, and poaching – even stealing a loaf of bread could lead to transportation.

The First Fleet

In May 1787, 11 ships set out from England, bound for Australia. On board were convicts, guards, officials such as judges, engineers and surgeons, and their families – 1,487 people in all. They arrived in Botany Bay on January 18, 1788, but discovered that the place was unsuitable for settlement. They sailed a short way along the coast and anchored at Port Jackson, in the heart of what is now Sydney, on January 26, 1788. This engraving of the time shows a chaplain blessing the convicts before departure.

A penal colony

Prison colonies were set up in areas other than Port Jackson. Port Arthur (shown below) in Tasmania became a much feared settlement. About 12,500 prisoners built a town there, parts of which still stand. The settlement was run in a harsh and brutal way, with much suffering and despair among the prisoners.

GOLD RUSH AND EXPLORATION

In 1851, gold was discovered in central New South Wales. Soon there were discoveries in Victoria, too. Thousands of Australians left their homes and farms and became gold prospectors in search of riches. They were joined by new arrivals from North America, Great Britain, and New Zealand, attracted by the prospect of quick and easy money. The reality for most was hardship and disappointment.

However, the gold rush led to a rapid expansion of Australia's tiny population. In the 10 years following 1851 the population grew from 405,000 to 1,200,000 (excluding the Aboriginals).

With a larger population and earnings from gold exports, the country quickly developed. Regular horse-drawn coach services were established, railroads and roads built, and telegraph lines erected. The settlers began to think of themselves as Australians, and became more aware of their country's identity, so there were increasing demands to gain independence from Great Britain. Between 1842 and 1900 each colony gained a right to self-government. The colonies became states, and in 1901 formed the Commonwealth of Australia, an independent country.

New arrivals
Among the many people who came to Australia in search of gold were the Chinese. About 42,000 arrived in Victoria alone during the first rush of immigrants. Many European-Australians resented the Chinese finding "their" gold and there were several riots. A landing tax for new arrivals was imposed by the states of Victoria, New South Wales, and South Australia. This slowed the numbers of Chinese entering the country. Many present-day Australians are descended from the Chinese families of this time.

The coach network
In 1853 Freeman Cobb brought the first stagecoaches from the U.S.A. and established a regular service transporting people to the goldfields. Within a few years a network of horse-drawn coaches, the buses of their day, was established throughout New South Wales and Victoria. As shown here, the mail was also carried by these coaches.

Ned Kelly's gang attack police in the outback, in about 1870

The Ned Kelly gang

From the 1860s, highway robbers on horseback held up coaches carrying gold and raided banks in gold-mining towns. They were called "bushrangers" because they hid in the outback bush lands. The most notorious bushrangers were Ned Kelly's gang, who wore suits of armor (shown above) to protect them from armed policemen. After years of robbery and murder, Kelly was finally captured and hanged in Melbourne in 1880.

Exploring the interior

The mid-1800s was the great age of exploration in Australia. Men such as Charles Sturt, Robert Burke, and William Wills suffered great hardship as they explored the lands deep in the interior, hoping to find great riches or perhaps even an inland sea. Burke and Wills were the first to cross the continent from south to north. But they perished through lack of food and water on their return journey, at their base camp at Cooper Creek.

Cooper Creek
Darling River
Murray River

Explorers' journeys

- Burke and Wills (1861-2)
- Charles Sturt (1830)
- Charles Sturt (1844-45)

GOVERNMENT AND CAPITAL

When Australia became a united, independent country in 1901, there were already plans to build a new national capital city. Its name was to be Canberra, from an Aboriginal word meaning "meeting place". The city's main plan was designed by an American architect, Walter Burley Griffin, in 1912.

Griffin planned a city for 25,000 people, but today Canberra is populated by more than 250,000. The design of the capital has allowed it to expand without overcrowding; the city is generally prosperous and the streets are wide and able to accommodate the busy traffic. In the suburbs, houses are well-spaced and fronted by green lawns. Massive tree planting has provided Canberra with shady cover from the summer heat, unlike most other Australian cities.

Since Griffin's time a war museum, art gallery, high court, library, university, and mint (where the nation's money is produced) have been built in Canberra. As the center of Australian government, Canberra has many government offices and more than 40 foreign embassies. It is also the home of the Australian prime minister and of the governor-general, who represents the ruling British monarch, who is also the monarch of Australia.

A veteran soldier proudly wears his medals on Anzac Day (see page 42) in commemoration of World War I.

The Wall of Wars

The War Memorial Museum in Canberra is visited by many thousands of Australians and tourists each year. The museum is a monument to those Australians who fought in the two World Wars, 1914-18 and 1939-45. An Honor Roll on an enormous wall records the names of the 102,000 Australians who died.

Captain Cook
Memorial Water Jet

Voyage globe

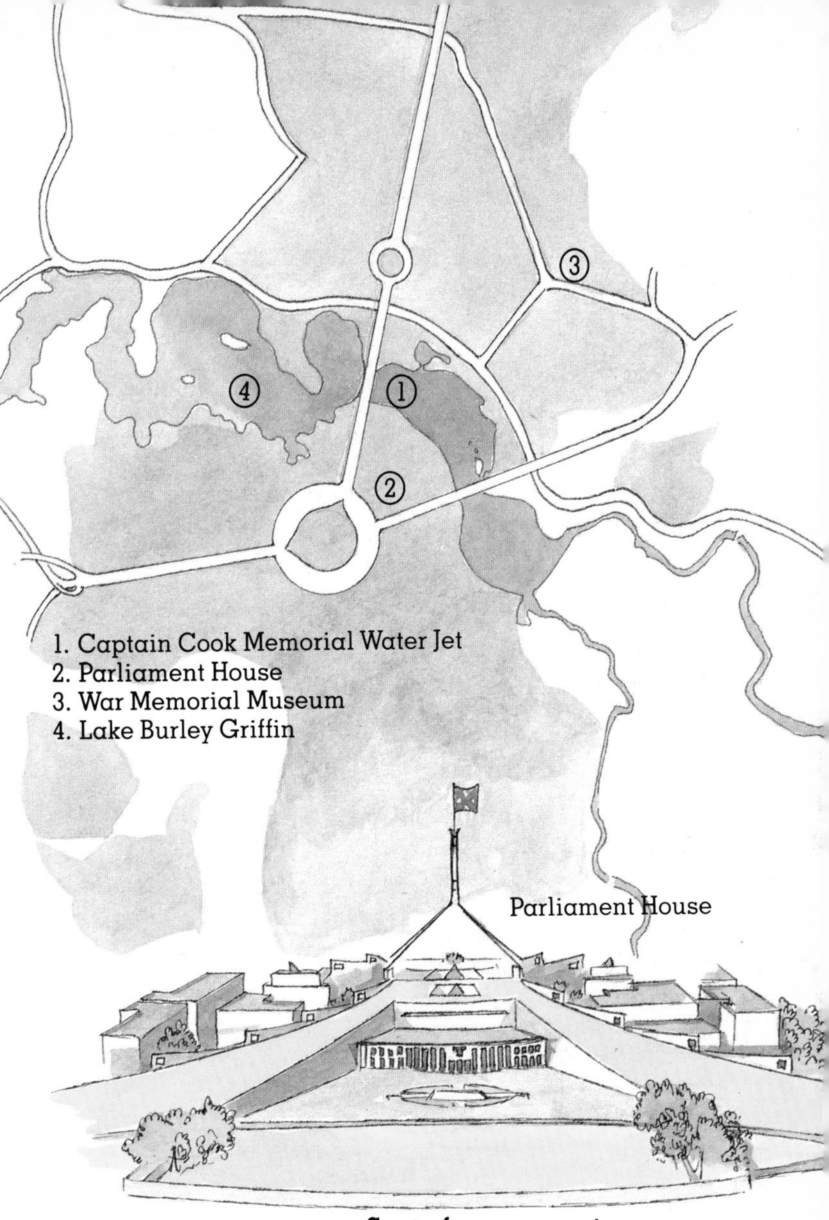

Griffin and Cook

The artificial Lake Burley Griffin, in the center of Canberra, is named after the city's architect. In the center of the lake is the Captain Cook Memorial Water Jet. The jet, one of the highest in the world, shoots water 460 feet into the air. There is a metal Voyage globe nearby, depicting the voyages made by Captain Cook around the world.

KEY FACTS

▶ Australia is a democracy. The people elect their government by voting. All Australians over the age of 18 must vote in general elections.

▶ There are two houses of Parliament, the Senate, or Upper House, and the House of Representatives, or Lower House.

▶ The Senate consists of 76 senators (12 from each state and two from each territory). Senators are elected every six years.

▶ Members of the House of Representatives are elected every three years. Their numbers are proportional to the populations of the states and territories.

Seat of government

The new Parliament House in Canberra opened in 1988, to coincide with Australia's Bicentennial celebrations. Above the main entrance is a frieze depicting events in Australia's history. The two houses of Parliament, the Senate Chamber and the House of Representatives, are linked by the Member's Hall. This has a pyramid-shaped skylight which fills it with natural light.

HARBOR AND OPERA

Sydney, with a population of three and a half million, is the largest city in Australia. It is also larger, in land area, than either New York City or London. Where the first settlers built their wooden shacks, mighty skyscrapers now stand.

Sydney is a bustling city, with many fine buildings, shopping centers, and places of entertainment. For the thousands of people who arrive in Australia each year, with the hope of starting a new and better life, Sydney is their first taste of their new homeland. It has a warm, sunny climate. Sunbathing, swimming, and surfing are the most popular outdoor pursuits. Sydney's beaches, such as Bondi (5 miles to the south), are favorite meeting places at weekends.

Next to Sydney Harbour Bridge is The Rocks, the oldest part of the city (see page 30). Although ravaged by fire and demolition, many old buildings remain. Some have been converted into fashionable shops, bars, and restaurants. The Rocks is probably unique in Australia because it has kept something of the atmosphere of the original European settlement.

Fun on the water
In Sydney Harbour, a natural harbor covering 200 square miles, boating and sailing are very popular. Each year on December 26 (Boxing Day) yachts set out on a race to Hobart, in Tasmania, as shown below.

Sails in the harbor
Sydney Opera House, opened in 1973, is one of the most striking buildings in the world. It was designed by Danish architect Joern Utzon and cost over $100 million. The Opera House consists of five main halls: a concert hall (seating 2,700 people), a drama theater (550 people), and the opera theater (1,500), a cinema (420), and a recording hall (300).

The Three Sisters
About 30 miles south of Sydney lie three prominent rocks known as the Three Sisters. They form part of the beautiful Blue Mountains, so-called because of the blue-tinted leaves on the many eucalyptus trees that grow there.

TODAY'S AUSTRALIANS

It has been said that Australia has the world's "newest" population. All present-day Australians, apart from the Aboriginals, are either descended from settlers over the past 200 years or have recently settled in Australia themselves.

Until 1945, many Australians referred to Great Britain as "home". This was because, until that time, most of the people entering the country came from the United Kingdom. Since World War II, people from many other countries have settled in Australia. Refugees from war-torn Europe came in search of a new beginning. In just three years, 1947 to 1950, one million people came to live in Australia. About half of these came from non-English speaking countries such as Italy, Greece, the Netherlands, Yugoslavia, and West Germany. Today, European settlers continue to make up the majority of the 100,000 people who come to settle in Australia each year.

Since the 1970s, many people from Asian countries have also settled in Australia. Some were refugees from Vietnam and Cambodia. Today's Australia is made up of many different peoples and cultures, as can be seen in the Italian, Arab, Chinese, or Vietnamese shopping areas in the major cities.

A taste of Italy
Restaurants selling all kinds of European food can be found in most Australian cities. Here an Italian restaurant owner gets ready for his next customer.

KEY FACTS

▶ More than three and a half million people have settled in Australia since 1945, making up one-fifth of the present total population.

▶ In spite of Australia's immense size, 85 per cent of its population live in cities and towns.

▶ Aboriginals or people of Aboriginal descent number about 160,000 today, about one-hundredth of the total population.

▶ Two million people, out of a total population of some 16 million, do not use English as their first language.

"China Town"
Large numbers of Chinese people emigrated to Australia during the gold rush. Both Sydney and Melbourne have their "China Town", an area packed with Chinese restaurants, bazaars, and food stores. Above is a typical street in Melbourne's China Town.

Happy families
The family is of great importance to the Australian way of life. Fine weather provides opportunities on weekends for families and friends to enjoy eating outdoors as here, and having a barbecue or "barbey". Almost a national summer tradition, steaks and other meats, fish, and vegetables are cooked on a charcoal grill, and washed down with ice-cold "tubes" or "tinnies" (cans) of lager beer.

SUN, SURF, AND SPORTS

With sunshine, warm weather, numerous parks, ample sports facilities, and an average 40-hour work week, Australians spend a lot of time outdoors playing and watching sports. In summer, swimming is the most popular recreation. Most Australian children learn to swim before they go to school; and Australian swimmers have excelled in international competition for many years.

Surfing, sailing, and water-skiing also are popular. In recent years windsurfing has become a craze. Australian tennis players, such as Evonne Goolagong-Cawley and Pat Cash, are known throughout the world. Cricket draws very large crowds in the summer, particularly the Test Matches played against other countries.

In the southern states, the two main participant sports in winter are various types of football and skiing. Soccer is the main type of football, but Rugby Union and Rugby League also are followed. In addition there is "Australian Rules" football, which is like a cross between rugby and soccer. More than 100,000 people watch the grand final in Melbourne each year.

Australian tennis player Pat Cash, winner of the Wimbledon men's single title in 1987

"Howz'at?"
Since Australians played their first Test Match against England in 1861, they have contributed many illustrious names to the game of cricket: Donald Bradman (possibly the greatest batsman the game has known), Richie Benaud, Dennis Lillee, and most recently, Alan Border. This picture shows Australian Test batsman Greg Ritchie in action at the Sydney Cricket Ground.

Sunburn and sharks

Swimming and sunbathing are the most popular Australian leisure pursuits, but they can be hazardous. For Australians with light, northern European skins, sunburn is not just uncomfortable, it can be dangerous. On many beaches swimmers would be prey for sharks if it weren't for "shark bars" which stop big sharks coming too close. Spotter planes also patrol beaches, and lifeguards, perched on top of a beach tower, keep a constant look out for hazards such as powerful surf and undercurrents as well as sharks. When red warning flags are flying on the beach, the message is simple: don't swim!

Surf and sails

Surfboard riding, above, is an all-time favorite Australian sport. Windsurfing is also very popular and is said to be easier to learn than surfboard riding. The boards and sails come in all sizes so even small children can become skilled in using them.

All at sea

In 1983 the Australian yacht *Australia II* (shown on the right) won the America's Cup yacht race, defeating the U.S. yacht *Liberty*. The nation celebrated the occasion in exuberant fashion. It was the first time in 132 years that the Americans had been beaten.

GROWING UP AN AUSTRALIAN

For all Australian children between the ages of five and 15 (16 in Tasmania), education is compulsory. Most children attend state schools, but about one in four of all school children attend private, mainly Roman Catholic, schools. At the age of 15 or 16 all children take a graduation examination. Those that do well may then go on to one of the 19 universities in Australia, or to one of many other colleges for further training. For children living in towns and cities, school life is much the same as for children in the United States.

Public holidays include two dates that are particularly Australian. The first is Australia Day (January 26) which celebrates the first European settlement in Australia over 200 years ago. The second is Anzac Day (April 25) which commemorates an event in World War I when Australia and New Zealand Army Corps (ANZAC) troops landed on the Gallipoli peninsula in Turkey. They aimed to capture Constantinople (now known as Istanbul), the capital of Turkey, Germany's ally. The landing was fiercely opposed and proved disastrous for the Anzac troops. Thousands died. It was a bitter blow to all Australians and has been commemorated ever since.

The flying doctor
Alice Springs is the home of the Flying Doctor Service. About 1,000 people from the interior of the country use the service. If they need medical treatment or advice they contact the "Flying Doctor" using their two-way radios, which have a range of 1,250 miles. If the illness or injury is not too serious, the doctor will prescribe medicine from the medical supplies kept in every isolated homestead. In more serious cases, an ambulance plane or helicopter is sent to bring the patient to a hospital. Only rarely does the doctor fly out to the patient. If this is necessary, however, an entire medical team is standing by, as shown here.

Anesthetist Surgeon Pilot

Living "out back"

For children living on a remote sheep farm, a visit to their friends "next door" may mean a trip of 60 miles. School lessons arrive by mail, or may be conducted over the air, via one of the 12 Schools of the Air. These give children two hours of two-way radio contact with a teacher (shown above) every day.

Higher education

Children who do well in the graduation exam may then go on to one of the 19 universities in Australia. Sydney University (its library is shown here) is the oldest, founded in 1850. There are also about 80 colleges of technology.

TOMORROW'S AUSTRALIA

In the 200 years since the first European settlers arrived in Australia, much has been achieved. The land has been cultivated and industries created; and Australians now have one of the highest standards of living in the world.

This has been achieved at a price, however. Australia's original inhabitants, the Aboriginal people, have suffered greatly. Aboriginal land rights and the welfare of the Aboriginals throughout Australia have both become major political issues.

In the past 30 years, Australia has become more involved with its neighbors in Southeast Asia and the Pacific. Aid is now given to countries like Papua New Guinea (which it once controlled). Yet, like other advanced industrial nations, Australia experienced increasing unemployment during the 1980s. Despite the country's enormous agricultural and mineral wealth, Australia still suffered from the downturn in industrial growth experienced by many other countries, especially those in Europe.

In the next 30 years, Australia may turn more and more toward Asia and the Pacific for its trading partners. No longer isolated "down under", few Australians will ever again think of themselves as migrants or descendants of families from Europe or Asia, but simply as Australians.

An Aboriginal first
Pat O'Shane, above, was the first Aboriginal woman to become a barrister (a type of lawyer). She was admitted to the Bar of Australia's Supreme Court in 1976.

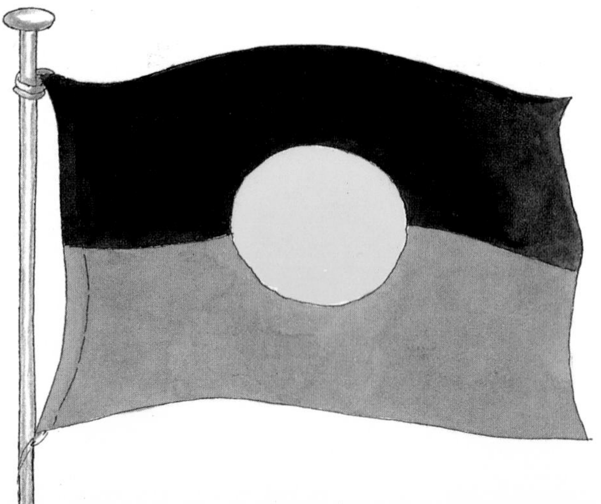

Fight for rights
The Aboriginal flag was designed by Harold Thomas, an Aboriginal artist, in 1972. It symbolizes their future: the people (black), the land (red), and the sun (yellow).

Caring for the land

In the years to come, Australia will earn much money from its vast reserves of metals, minerals, and gemstones. But huge mining developments, such as this one near Coober Pedy, are destroying the landscape. There is a growing awareness that Australia's land, and its unique wildlife, must be conserved. The pig-footed bandicoot (right) is one of several small Australian marsupials that has lost out to the cats, dogs, mice, and rats brought by the settlers. Like more than a dozen similar creatures, it may already be extinct.

Index

Acknowledgments
All illustrations by Ann Savage.
Photographic credits (*a* = above, *b* = below, *m* = middle, *l* = left, *r* = right): Cover *al* Smith/Zefa, *bl* Promotion Australia (London), *ar* All-Sport, *br* G Ricatto/Zefa; page 9 Australia News & Information Bureau; page 10 New South Wales Dept of Tourism; page 11 Jean-Paul Ferrero/Ardea; page 12 *a* Australia Information Service, *b* Promotion Australia (London); page 15 cover; page 17 Heather Angel; page 19 *a* cover, *b* Promotion Australia (London), *b* Jean-Paul Ferrero/Ardea; pages 22 and 23 Promotion Australia (London); page 24 Australia Information Service; page 25 Promotion Australia (London); page 26 J M Start/Robert Harding Picture Library; page 27 Chris Fairclough/Colour Library; page 28 Hutchison Library; page 29 Baglin/Zefa; page 31 The Mansell Collection; page 33 ET Archive; page 36 Promotion Australia (London); page 37 *a* cover, *b* Croxford/Zefa; page 38 Victoria House; page 39 *a* Bernard Regent, *b* Commonwealth Institute Library (Compix); page 40 *a* All-Sport; page 41 *a* cover, *b* Promotion Australia (London); page 43 *a* Compix, *b* Promotion Australia (London); page 45 K E Job/Hutchison Library.